MIRTH

MIRTH

Linda Russo

chax press

Tucson 2007

Cover image: *Loaves & Fishes*
© 2007 by Gwyneth Scally
Used with permission of the artist.

Printed in the USA.

Chax Press / 101 W. Sixth Street / Tucson, Arizona 85701-1000 / USA

ISBN 978-0-925904-63-8

To the editors of the following publications among whose pages portions of this book in some version appeared I wish to express my gratitude:

BoogLit Postcards ("Here is love and peace"); *Buffalo Vortex* ("'Photoillustration of Martha's last laugh' and 'post-attack'" and "I Know a Man"); *Colorado Review* ("text/The closed writes the poem . . . ,""a style not my own/The odor is unapologetic . . .," "strict confidence/I'm sorry if I have let you down. . ."); *Chicago Review* ("'Wars,' he remarked. . .," "Arms & Violent wars . . ." "what I am saying applies to both . . ." "this I should not say, but I will . . .," "Still, if you want to be well. . .," "I corrected my itemized list of faults," "This is the tale of battle . . ."); *ecopoetics* ("Again. A gain and a lost loss..." and "It is one thing to see..." from "Achilles' Helix"); Elevator Books, *Postcard Project* (2001) ("what I meant to lose was . . ."); *endnote* ("How do I look?," "I make my own marks" (formerly "Americanity"), "will I do what for what for what?" (formerly "You need new shoes . . ."), "Otherness tells the same story . . ." (formerly "Studying Hunger")); *Jacket* ("I was a doctor, and sick . . .," "perfecto fiesta," "gender mark-down," ("I make my own marks..."), "It's a boy and It's a girl," " 'Photoillustration of Martha's last laugh' and 'post-attack' ," "Here is love and peace," "My biggest problem . . .," "don't do or say that to that"); *Pinstripe Fedora* ("Exactness"); *Plantarchy* (" 'wiggles plus moans'," " 'his ideological'," "How do I look?," "India Day Theme Song"); *There* ("an air," "asnooze in the pallid light of reality").

MIRTH was written in Buffalo, NY and Norman, OK, between 2000 and 2006, and on a plane to Oakland, CA in March of 2005. I'd like to thank Chris, Kaplan, Kirk, Jessica, Lauren, and Eleni for their friendship and camaraderie over the years. And for my initial encoding, I owe many thanks my parents (and the powerlines of ConEdison).
I would also like to extend a special thank you to Charles Alexander for making this publication possible.

This book is dedicated
to fellow citizens.

Something echoed inside Connie: 'Give me the democracy of touch! The resurrection of the body!' She didn't know at all what it meant, but it comforted her, as meaningless things may do.

D.H. Lawrence, *Lady Chatterly's Lover*

Contents:

Intersection Heartland

There, with dizzy attention, I hold the because,
another key to the bewitchment of words.

—Rosmarie Waldrop, *The Reproduction of Profiles*

Exactness

she said o she's just closing her eyes because she's bored they laughed was
something wrong? by now the other had gone into the other room they stood
in a way that didn't warrant response their two faces were pushed together
attached with unnatural smiles it reminds me of the bribe, she said that keeps
them awake their response was palliative, agreeable and awkward it eased her
into a position of tempered regret the cold feet surely had at their root a
disorder of the highest order the truth shot out of her body limpid glue

they took what was offered she said it recalled the botched assault they looked
askance their breasts were pushed together in emphasis raising their
awareness without them in sexual confusion bodies rolled on the floor
yet everything was in its place

provocative images were laid bare she said it was liable, or pliable in unison
their pinched looks dissolved was her predisposition apt? date rape
reached an all-time low others moved out of the room to exchange assertions
pushed their thighs together fluids were shared in a way that suggested controversy
though the offending document remained that evening clothes flew off

I won't know the result of my campaign, she said they twisted in their seats to
satisfy an itch the literacy issues remained the others admitted their love
of malice went unmet her shoulder squinched up to her teeth to receive a bite
that was the end of the meeting

sipping coffee he lost control of the car with a gradual movement their
shoulderblades met was it likely to ignite discussion? she insisted, then
she broke off completely that's it the essential history canonized

"Wiggles Plus Moans"

She is wiggles plus moans [or means]

in an apiary plot
[or topiary]

to defeat terrorists through urban renewal

surplus statisticus
& spell-binding beautification

unlearning football will be our downfall
oh, that makes me bellow, fellows

whose cheeks are fresh
whose minds are fresh

"His Ideological"

Let's kick out
his ideological
video image

the weather prediction
comes back negative

the nouveau riche returning to India

the senate drafts his ideological exclusion provision

we're back to the bottle full throttle
we've made up with our minds against
we've learned crafts we've earned independence of pieces of minds
we're earsplugged
we've rates of transmission

we honest gropers need spastic plastic digits

else what you want

How do I look?

When I look into your eyes
I realize yours are not eyes at all
but windows.

Okay?

(Let us not speak of the past.)

India Day Theme Song

this leisurely pace, the quiet room is killing me

remind me, again, where I am

democracy's kitchen souped-up with lobbyist sit-ins

Take only one – only
under pressure can I, dear, be me

Go ahead, I'll pay for dinner, mix and sweeten in post-production,
I'll admire my shell in the pharmaceutical gleam in your eye.

Not knowing what I'm looking for I can't explain.
I can't feel my sentence.

Let's share technology while I establish safeguards and show the world they don't understand – the people just have to understand! You just have to understand!

Pride is the fearless financing of crimes:

Carbomb in Carachi – that's catchy.

Seeking inspiration in others' books, we benefit.

Indira day or Sandra Day. India needs more energy.

"Asnooze in the Pallid Light of Reality"

In the heat of the night of violence & investment principals

caca dia do
praise god early and often

educational access squarepants design

spin spin
no downpayment
practice
practice, practice

His piercing pinched eyes and pinched nose success story
make women want to make it with him

they're a part of the architecture of social provision

peep squawk

paid news asnooze in the pallid light of reality chat

profits skyrocket priorities

commercial instinct windbreak

Daily Buzz

Good Morning

take the number of demands we have placed on the Chinese government
& multiply for each time it's recalled
we've not signed the nuclear non-proliferation agreement
subtract the Iraq thing from the other day
divide Iran by Middle East Peace Talks & multiply the sum by that percentage
then raise to the power of Canada

What did you get?

I got three new genders.

I got irredeemable self-interest as the locus of poetic inspiration

my net worth nets no words

My total deductions : 892 dollars 98 cents & my credits were 167
dollars 37 cents
my standard deduction : 5000 dollars
my total tax : 1751 dollars 63 cents & my expected refund is 128
dollars 89 cents
my routing number : 221 868 474; account number 000986943102

My intake astounds no one

I will curry favor to no one, no matter

I pose in front of my property

I will not mention the state of my hands, or your hands,
but I will suggest Bert's Lemon Cuticle Butter
for your toe nails. You should really consider
doing something about that.

We need not
exist for
the profit-
driven industry
that feeds on
normal
unpretty
everyday sort of
people
like us

The poem, however, the poem, the poem, the poem

Hello.

Strategies for Anxiety Cure

It's not just that your friends annoy me.
I haven't had a proper breakfast
for thirteen years. If we
don't keep up with current events
are they current? My toes, also pink, stink.
Under our system the statesman has such status.
I am an island, I am a rock, and fragrant, and my strategies
for sadness are none of your business.
Here's something we can all chew on. Pork is still
the other white meat. But could we just hold each other?
In the dream it persisted. Though canned ham is cured.
I can't tell you where I'm going with this.
I'm not lonely – I'm just getting restless!
I don't see any ships or waves. Or casseroles.
I have not been on my knees like the chore
demands. I just can't get myself to do it, I'm a fear factor
failure straight from the disposition factory. Who am I
kidding? I have not been on my knees or asked to get on my knees.
No one actually said my boobs were all wrong.
I shouldn't swear. I do.
Is this the right skirt? Does it look right on me?

I. Jessica Simpson Ethics Video Pitch

I'm just trying to matter too.
But your assumption is not body model

perspicacity

two bright cardinals lock beaks,
fly vertical in a real ordeal

news delivers rotating cities of destruction

to the president – my cleavage rebuff

I gather my absurdities, your hopes among them
daily

II. Ethics Recovery Program

"Stainless is more... elegant." *www.geappliances.com*

I can see now that
sexuality, and stupidity
the model was not accurate
my mind returns to the bristling place
of polished steel appliances
cooling my fevered cheek

"Photoillustration of Martha's last laugh" and "post-attack"

Martha Stewart's face on some Teutonic body
what are the boundaries in the case involved?
it's her future that illustrates the angle on the story
and the joke is that much the richer without intending to
deceive but to muse and for that we've gotten regrettable attention
we were too successful a little too successful
attempts at economic destruction will not work
investments and businesses would be devastated
consumer confidence would plunge
the deficit would sky rocket
another attack would scare bank rollers
let's make the economy resilient to another attack
faster clean up would boost consumer confidence
let's make the economy resilient to another attack
let's plan to clean up faster to boost consumer confidence
let's send a clear message
an attempt at economic destruction will fail

An Air

Relax your throat. Intimate boundaries constructed of air, the moving eye, the powerful, disturbed. I suppose. They watch. Let's not let them let us. It's what they want. It's their power over me. My social service as botoxic. It's simply astonishing. To have such power is . . . I earned it. What can I say. Privilege is a burden I earned. My fans love it. I'd throttle myself if I could. I'm that happy.

I myself am a huge fan of air: noise, emissions control, wind energy, kite flying, flag waving, and cloud watching. And breathing! You name it. I love a conflict! Sometimes you have to choose – flags or demanding tougher standards for industry? It's a small sacrifice, but we make it. Superb. Breathe. Relax your throat! Throw your shoulders back. Visualize your lungs as expanding helium grapes! You are floating. You and your angel face – you know that?

If there are good forces and evil forces only, then we can just forget about the evil. It runs its course and History proves it. The subtle campaign to intimidate academics should cease. We need history – I mean we're here, aren't we? It's a grand plan, you have to admit, that I am here, and you are here, and I know you're not evil. I do. I do. I do. I've eradicated it, personally.

I didn't mean to make you cry, or feel slighted, or inadequate, or unloved, or crying, bawling, spitting up, smelling of vomit. I certainly didn't mean to procreate, and now I'll have spit up all over my breasts, which used to be so pristine. I mean they were tidy and now look at them. No don't. My stupid cat just licked a bug. She's not fit to eat that! Stupid cat! I want you to cheer up!

Consider this: the average American woman will spend over 400 days of her life shopping for the perfect pajamas – yet is she happy? Does the shopping cease?

If I could say one thing about my country I would say that it's stupid that I only get to say one thing.

How did I get here?

Jingle for the Rising Cost of Health Care

It's a marketing blitzkrieg and fat kids have no fun.

Childhood *is* overwrought.

Out of control.

For example, I once wanted & went global as stars are, like razor blades,
and as sketchy. *That was my creed*, with hopes for a better appraisal,
it was based on the friendly fire coming my way in the form of the happy.

The seats were cold & bright & superstar & that made us feel special.

That's smart. Who cares who got off on selling out?
We do.
We still do.
Wee all still do!

Ears piqued like stars all night our nation anthems.

Domestic Clean-up Campaign Rally Song

Random genetics fling me a brat.
I muss up dinner, they export potential
diners to Egypt for torture and clean plates –
my palate's got a bad taste in it – in the tradition of our reign.

Opulent, sinister, and cold.
Where's the bling in that? It's all mannerisms.
What are the effects of expression of oppression in a language the people
understand?

What's wrong with you people? Hold hands.
My harbinger flip flops in morse code:
"I'm sorry. I said I'd protect
the United States, and look at this mess, my words

"work like chants
my darn boots fitted backward
better. I say smack them down,
the decider I am."

Super Important Political Content

It gives me great pleasure to address the stairwell.
In this case I would like to support
the suggestion that
we recognize abortion
as a symptom
of an unforgiving
system.

The importance in, and a target of, a source.

Shoot out, seize the proper
noun my high forehead radiates
skin supplies   must get skin supplies
  an attractive sac, a noble bone, the humble
aspiration to be

        none of this is headed in the right direction,

                zealots,

forward profits to fund alternatives
the moral compasses
my many sugar piechart

A Salve

That's not what I meant!

Let's hear it for
the captains of industriousness and their right
to undo my geography.

In my dream my dreams of mastery were dashed.
Too err is female, to forgive, naught.
'Tis pink and fleshly and mobile.

TV news makes me bawl.

The uniform lack of self-appraisal,

the unrelenting hair get-ups, the flat faces of information

feed.

The dream of common knowledge deferred?

The skinny critique.

I think I would know you in a crowd. I would know you,
and not only that, I would love you. I would love you, and
I would lick you all over, and you would like that! You want
my love don't you. You like that.

Folksong for the Midwestern Masses

If I had a hammer and a sail
the wind would.

Dust had, either way,
both matter.

One way at once
bulbs burn and billow.

Radiant sails, onward,
mind turning jade (on sale at Pier One).

A hot rock for comfort.
Hammer smash settee.

When I am stone cold sink
fathomable darkness flammable shirt,

politics like cork,
gender to cover

your thighs like the downy,
cattleroving tracks not footprints – but the whale will.

Remedies of Love

Love read the name of this book
before I had written a sentence

—Ovid

Dark green – loving the ground –
am I a victim of love
    I have no body to sing of
what can I do in these lines
do we give in –

seen them die, swell lines

"Wars," he remarked, "I can see clearly are waiting for me."
"O Stupid," I said in reply, "some young men, sometimes, are cold."

I am no traitor, no renegade, no turncoat, no consequence, no determinant, no science, no deserter, no newer than a muse's navel turned fresh to a happy fire, to sail on favorably, then pleasurably, to keep moving.

O Stupid, lover of armory & courting disharmony, you killer, you, disenamored, an
        enemy.
I declare, and what am I doing now? I am loving.

And some poor wretch made a rope of his collar.

Thousands the forms of disease, thousands the methods of cure.
There is a forgetfulness there.

Arms & Violent wars & meter suited to make it matter.
Arms & Violent wars, all in hexed meters to measure
a matter my foot's too small. I meander, preparing
to sound, all in a thrall that's bewitching
when here comes Stupid snickering
one foot big as oil.

"Why you bad boy!" I said, "who gave you jurisdiction?"
My lines rose well in lofty measure
but his lines next corrupted the text.

I make my own marks girl-kind I'm little girls she's sexy like that like an identity I fit myself into like deployment it's optional like pill

A girl's sexy with arms twice sexy not right and left just two not parity but bi-party the girl her charms she uses her arms like levers like digits like machines we vote in moving us forward and into the back

Past-ward low-tech-like like still phallic intern sex she's good with her arms

This is the tale of battle between the lover and the door.
The door does not open to admit the lover. Let the lover curse,
let him kick the door, bribe the guard, let him all golden burn,
jeweled and deluded, let his curses be like poison to
the unmoving door. It's a funny tale because no one dies, and the door
doesn't care, and the lover is only inflamed because he loves,
and lovers only break through doors in the night time, and
nights only shorten. Time is running out, like an arms
inspection. He wants what's on the other side, otherwise he'd recover,
and the let the door be a door, and not his foe.

No powerhouse here. No great lore. Just getting along the striations
of your long long lashes – a kind of love that leads your tips to greatness,
to which they belong.

will I do what for what for what?
you need new shoes and I need a new disposition
either way we're the same good citizenry
harboring a revenge fantasy, that's one good advantage over me
naming your price

the rate of exchange across my peeking navel

Some, I know, complain that my muse is a whore.
Whoever they are they should know:
hexameter verse can't deal with the pleasures of love.
They should learn at least this much:
The world is public
to my conspicuous mark.
I go where I please. That is my art.
To cast signs and return them
never saying a word
spelling out words, making
signs. My licentious offense is to tell.

I was a doctor, and sick, and really desperate. The only thing that did any good was the most repetitious insistence on every one of my faults, which brought effective relief. I said "look at my ugly legs" though some would say they weren't ugly at all. I said "what a cunt!" "How demanding!" and there was a trace of truth in that, and yet people called me Un-American. I could not even tell them apart, what I was and what they scorned me to be. I had full round breasts but deemed myself *fat as a pig* or I had slack breasts and refused myself a bra; I was articulate but spat at myself *stuck-up* and *bitchy*; I was simply good but labeled myself *fool*. I waddled and took myself out walking. I had crooked teeth and told myself a funny story, I had a sorrowful tale to flood my watery eyes. I surprised myself many a morning when I wasn't ready, I did this on purpose to catch myself when I wasn't expecting a call, I caught myself smelly and ugly, with bad breath and bad hair and a bad complexion, and saw more to myself that way than I'd ever seen. They called me a critic and meant I was a rat, they called me a witch and knew not what they meant, and that helped me to see I had not been mistaken. I came unforeseen, victim and failure and danger and vixen and fraud. Because there hides the essence of love.

Men she could change into beasts –
Those she could not change – they
Wait

Still, if you want to be well, it must be endured
bitter tonics cold placebos straight gates terrible trials first galls drastic
ailments private accounts army comforts girly comrades external reviews fire
attacks irksome bits wretch excuses
            steely, thirsty swift cinches
fierce with implacable arms

Lovers of profit are still at war

For want of something to take
hold of me
I went out and bought
a new dress
such is the danger of daughters

Lovers of profit are still at war

this notice has startled the grass

to our relief, and a meager portion of trouble
Lovers of profit are still at war

I knew another man, who, rapidly running away, found remembrance.
If you don't want to love, a young friend of mine once said,
don't expose yourself.

I corrected my itemized list of faults,
listen to me while I sing
sleepfulness, randomness, rambling, slouching, befuddlement
I clip wings, I am grown
I know the signs, I explain my decisions
There are reasons to explain
waves, and the river, and the lachrymose
are reasons

my counsel is sound
the words of my mouth are girl cold

Otherness tells the same story again and again of a quiet girl bent over
a desk but with shorter sentences and the hemline inching up and down like
the yo-yo I am thinking I go through life and that's my punishment
to bend my ass into the shortest possible sentences

Like sentiment next to cement like the whiter teeth I want or the vast indifferent
bloom of my pink and airbrushed – this too must be counted among them

That's when it's clear the assumptions are made despite (you, me, it, our) most
gracious denials

Here is love and peace
except that I am wounded
and have no faith.
I want to be taught in the school,
like a scholar, to itemize
my booty, but I'm much too nice to
be bothered and besides
I am wounded
and troubled and
delighted and aroused and appalled.

need not have taken to rape, need not have taken
nine desperate ways to the sea, need not have changed to a bomb
need not have taken a bull for a lover, need not have watched
from the top of a tower ships spreading sails to their wind
need not have razed in a doom, need not have read books and written
need not have made ruinous, need not a ram or a wand
there is no difference now.

What I am saying applies to both.

What I meant to lose was
presentiment, embarrassment
What I promised to give was
immediate recrimination
What I expected to gain was
potential embarrassment
What I strove for was
given. What I vaunted
was going. What I mastered
was experiential, was gone. What I ceded
was real and rare. Embarrassment.

What I intended to lose was embarrassment.

Letters read over and over again helped to cure me. I know.

note:

Ovid's *The Art of Love* (from which "Remedies of Love" takes its epigraph) consists of four books: The Loves – The Art of Beauty – The Art of Love – The Remedies for Love. In a time of peace (2 or 1 B.C.), with no war to chronicle, Ovid turns his attention toward society (although the state is never far from his mind). He is a keen observer and a witty, sometimes biting but never loveless commentator, except where women are concerned: his comments regarding the arts of seduction and what he calls "remedies," cures for unwanted desires or desirers (always female) are blatantly misogynistic.

"Remedies of Love" makes its ground, for the most part, in a 1957 translation by Rolfe Humphries that, attempting to preserve Ovid's original meter and line length, results in a somewhat "contemptible throng"(I.6).

"Remedies" commenced during the lead-up to the United States' invasion of Iraq in 2003. It is prompted by the question of how one (female) enters into the histories and discourses of these sacred theatres – ancient war, cold war, contemporary war – international in scope yet keenly inscribed upon the most intimate domestic details of our everyday lives.

Achilles' Helix

Buffalo NY, 2000-2004

love
is the substance I am most
which releases
me not from
the body
but from its en-
culturation
    Alice Notley, "Office"

If she exists, to sit here in words quiet wonder. Does she exit the page and into another dimension. Clinging to clanging. Makes space. A hunger spun.

Your charms, an odor ineffably you caught in a weave, that is your writing. Does she exit the cloth and come clean.

The odor is unapologetic. The texture commands we up- or a-braid our bottoms. The luminescence dully awaits shears. The size sings its singularity in all sizes. The appropriate pattern seizes your eye. Dizzily.

A light. Shines through words, what speaks out of a life, minutes captured and transformed, projected onto matter, a cracked reference to see through tint. A humor I know little of. A bile made apparent. One beat then two beats. One of another member remembers. Whistling around a corner. Pink machine.

Again. A gain and a lost loss. A can opened to nourish. A hunger spin, a sore spine curled.

Bell. Bong. Teeth. Chatters. A record of mental wellness. Because you so seldom spoke of pique and so seldom speak of poke. A weedy inheritance.

A love struck occurrence, a currency. Swift. Shot through with. Quiet. A propeller broken spoken. A noise of another banged. From a convexity (love) with a spoon. The little sleeps and dreams. A basic breed. A greed. Advanced, encouraged, redlined like hot sex in papers. Echoed in buildings, personages. A need by design.

The house not cleaned on a bi-weekly basis. A cycle recycled and through, till worn through. A week in sentences a month in syllables. A morning every morning by car. A dying caught up with. Atrophy spent in exhaust. A liver bothered to filter. A shoulder tender for one's own tears.

It is one thing to see quite another to be seen. To relate. Relish the late. Hour of quiver. A momentary leaf to a screen. To hide loves sad biddance. Clear bareness.

That lovely soup recipe. For tonic add tears and admonish.

Or hear a willing tree and leave. A willing sky and leave. A blue willing. A color named cobalt. A salt taken for balance. Growing upward and outward. A singularly uniform. Expression of the inside hung out. Sex me. As a tree.

Which means she has choices? Banging as a way into song, into sugar intact as a substance, clinging tongue. Clang or cling? Grope or cling? Fall short or misbehave? Which means she has choices?

I become indeterminable long after the meaning made clear to me the advantage of such a determination. I became not determined to love or find satisfaction or even to keep my house. I determined this after much study of facts, which are consequences. With a particular noise your car makes. I will always be startled by that whistle one day before I found it was you. That placed me and made me airy a minute, then solid.

I deter the usual information about myself. I am more than a collection, a datum. I have needs like data switching off and on in me. Like the refrigerator motoring on and off to nowhere. A destination of degree. It needs juice and I need juice, and to dissolve in you occasionally. This way to swallow. Bits so constituent such that it hurts too much not to be loved by you. And by you. And by all of you.

A motor running under my tongue. Along the shaft and soft under belly. A peek under the girlhood. Smashing mouthy must. Smitten with my ear to your globe. Inside your soft anger fixes. Hides its grace. Its givenness. A trait like a crack. You can't trace. Only inherit. The mouth you are in a battle to be forgiven with. That is never a triumph.

The closed writes the poem from without the dictionary. The open casts its eye to spread thighs. The closed smashed tongue against teeth. Vs. an unmeasured mixture of mythologies. The closure the inclusion of its own instructions. The aperture asks the hand to machine.

I heard the cough and the shuffle of feet that means someone nearby is also not merely apparent. It's silly I know to reduce it to that. But more plausible than to select a particular attitude or posture as a standard of presence. Or to picture you walking up the drive. You bear instead a continual regress or recidivism. Which is not your fault or any indication of your constitution. Rather that I wish it were opposite – not of what is which is what I don't know – but of something imaginable. If I have lost your love I could get it back. That sort of infallible.

The lake of your eyes or someone else's eyes. The lack of eyes. A fruitful contingency rings.

An autumn day ripe with sunlight. As a sort of gratitude. As a clatter. As a witness. The trouble I'm in. And the way I wait.

How else but to imagine the invisible props of discourse or a labyrinth continually shifting in design that nonetheless leads me onward. The advantage is walls that approach only ankles, yet I trip. Though it look small I forget to myself the magnitude of my restriction. I wanted a labyrinth of warm soapy water. That is what I wanted instead of what got taken away from me. I was always a research assistant or was myself the source of facts. My toes formed the basis of an early assignment. That is how I began … to build … these tiny … walls.

Keep squirting reason in my direction and I'll oil its tiny hinge. I'll caress it lovingly as a hinge that bites might receive my caresses on that tiny part where it cannot bite and I will consider whether it were brass or lavender or to be much less exact, which is flesh. I smell you on me so it is tragic to think that I will soon forget you. And that my genes in their preparation will remember you into my skin. As we have shifted about in here to accommodate your possibility.

That I was a we, at least, to be in when I wasn't in language.

Solvency

for Robert Creeley

sol•vent (s•l•v•nt, sôl•-) *adj.* **1.** Able to meet financial obligations. **2.** Capable of dissolving another substance, – *n.* A substance, usu. a liquid, capable of dissolving another substance. [< Lat. *solvere*, loosen.] – **sol•ven•cy** *n.*

Impossible to say,
but there is no doubt
the skill the poet possessed was employed
for a sometimes almost overwhelming
pictorial effect –

a world wanted.
Unadorned.

An age that is peaceful, and law-abiding,
makes dull reading – the intention is
to destroy the entire human race.

This is one of the things we learn
from Ovid, and
continue to learn
from his ilk, till we come at length
to another war, and the usual
epic invocation of heaven's aid, and
straightaway an account of the origin
to dim a chaotic mass

organic juice, and sudden radiation.
people overconfident about the future
of management.
nipple exposure, and conventional wisdom.
awash in fluoride, and pleased fans.
American, and baseball, and ghosts, and.
an awesome holy man.
people anticipate a rise in value, and purchase.
conservatism, and a thinning flock.
politics, and confidence.
stability, and the bigger picture.

PERFECTO FIESTA

my party
that made
me cry - - -

it's my
dress they
demand
and
the way
the sway
demands

Big social justice or big securities fraud?

Eternal promise – or they make us eternal – make us
bend till we've met – like contortionists?

Let's share toys. Let's pretend we're susceptible to private bids and ownership.

Hatch a profit? Or hatchet benefits – ?
You go ahead now preen for your entrance.

You rock or you roll
I will bombshell

I'll admit I wanted to imagine the ending
You might consider me a natural disorder
We can see eye to eye if we see what they see

being lining, muscled inside like preponderance
out of joint and errant, on dozens
and readily, physically
removing herself, to be certain as a stain is,
to obviate, prepared to remain conciliate
in discord or concord, fecund
without a doubt itinerant, in and
out of, in spite of, given in to, kinetic

a desire is different
you can turn it on when you want it
when exposed, my sexuality came to terms with my violence

sentiments?
framed as such
accidents, and
the feelings are loose,
in danger of intoxification

television, like an inoculation, exposed me

perk it or work it
warm it up, I *know* it

I, who meant what she said, who
won't stand for it, and
will run with it or
what else can it

List your lexicon. Compare. Categorize. Compare.
In construction your sentences bear in mind the
perpetuity of action. Every word a verb, and spoken.
A plan sketched out, planar.
A contradiction on paper. A thoroughly remastered
and temporary inclusion – as all sentences are
to the mind; which is to speak to our only detriment.

Unless augmented:
do your selfhelp seeking in the form of archaeology, a classic
explanation with loopholes, exceptions.

When I was girl
as can be
with legs I was
hot
a trooper
I did this
without having
to say
I was
without having to ask
I was other . . .

Hero, kiss me or I die!

movies, as analogies, are easy
to transform a too-peaceful age
into an ordered whole

as yet unfit for publication
but aburst in melodrama fueled by faith and
a change in the way a broadcaster operates

caught in the crossfire of culture wars
at risk of angering viewers
who would likely be familiar, naturally

it was never intended
to be final, to solve
the problem of the real intention –

exile, and the possibility of destroying the poem

I only say it to indicate my thinking
Forgive me for having that word with you
We can't help but have this (and that) in common

but it is different, ardent, an habitual haloed farewell
in a hardened glow, a hermetic vehement against
the breath being entirely her (own)
vim or nil, in her entirety numinous – like the counted coin
she will be missed, suspect, imagined
the one with the trace

tipalet

*

typical
trash
topical
biohazard

everyone want a piece of it

*

don't throw
it out
without
a doubt - - -

it's our
space
station
demands
damnation - - -

*

all want it girl-like

is a mouth
a speech
of holes?
and words full?
I heard *fill* or *fille*

then what?

I can on occasion
face it momentarily,
my place

all drops into it,
falls, or
going to eventually

This waiting is awful. It's worse
than that. It's the worst, the awfulest.
This waiting is the worst, it's horrible,
it's worse than that, awfully so,
it's terrible. This waiting is horrible.
It's endless, it's worse than that.
It's horrible, terrible. Just awful.
Terrible, just terrible: endless,
simply endless and awful, horrible
and ghastly. The horriblest, awfulest
ghastliest. It's worse than that.
It's more horrible, more terrible.
This waiting is unbearable.
It's awful. Just terrible. Horrible.
Ghastly. It's worse than that.
It's unbearable.

I.

I approach with such
I called her across
the room – I cannot
I cannot see you

I can see you
I can't – I could
climb a mountain – I
could look at – I

did not expect you
I didn't – I don't
hate you lately – I
don't –

If.
. . . if I can –
If I can't hope
then to hell with
it – If it ever

is – If it falls
flat – If I were
you – If the water
forms – If we are
to exist – If we

go back to where
If you – If you
never do anything for

anyone else – If you
wander far enough – If
you were going to

III.

I had wanted a
quiet testament – I have
come far enough – I
have never – I keep

to myself such – I
knew where they were
I know a man
I know two women

I'll miss the small
birds that come

How thin the love that acts according to prosperity, how pliant in its own standard of acquiescence. It's too dark and too unwieldy and too unlike love. It's heavy.

I'd rather the past were a series of errors or
you'll have to account for the flaws
The thing we want now is currently offered

being tropic, specifically charged
glue, as difficult to read as handwriting is
unplumbed, unsounded, not agitated
calm, probably, agreeable
and veritable, as a real or genuine stranger is
yours, your sight of surrender
like a sound was that sent her

I think you are misreading (it, me, the text, she)
threw a book against a wall as a way to err
bits of paint clarified a blow occurred
a painted bowl stood in for her
a standing army rushed to pierce her doubt

stay clear? stay clear? stay clear?

She was on my way and had forgotten to say where
a willful syntax reveals no fear
was her mouth full of bees?
feeling licked you pressed for answers, recognition

is what you'll achieve in the end
how many times had you imagined this outcome?

because the rest had fallen I made my bed
though I sleep in it now the sheets are not pressed
despite the pressure to close I pin my hope
my pinafore broach and a badge
a badge that said courage and was red like the pinpricks we bore as a badge

we had Wanted too much it is certain we were far too certain it is sure sure
we wanted we wanted we wanted?

where I was too callous or where I demurred I was too much engaged
at that moment to mean as words do

Some Say

Some say
you have not simply
insisted on yourself. You
have always wanted
to be friends, to be
one of many

and never to argue
the irrelevance
of anyone else.

Some are persuaded that
life even
in its largeness
might be manageable
brought round and
made soft

that to care, you
try to make it
care with your humble, illiterate
and awkward gestures.

So you thought,
the inevitable,
 some loved you,
some.

You waited for
some wind
to lift, some
thing to happen,
proving, it finally

making sense more than the literal,
still separate.

a road, a leaf of
the dropped tree
some location in place

everything put wordly-like
in its weightiness

how is that again

the slower purposeful
all that pushed to the side
and lifted with the uplifting finding of

a sustainable society
other animals of different kinds

and the choices we had to make at every stage in the process were difficult
there were a truly astonishing number of outstanding candidates – demonstrating the remarkable vitality of the field
difficult choices had to be made
we were impressed by the considerable talents of our applicants, but our particular needs led us to interview those candidates whose range of talents best match our needs at this time
we received an unusually large number of applications, and the selection process was particularly difficult
decisions such as these are always difficult to make, and I hope you will not consider the result a sign of any specific weakness in your credentials or your work
working with a large and talented pool of applicants
while your credentials are very impressive, we have chosen a candidate whose work experience and education are closer to our needs
our decisions were largely based upon whether candidates would be a good fit for our needs, and thus you should not perceive the fact that you were not included as a reflection of your abilities
the response to our ads for the position was overwhelming
the overall quality of the applicants was striking and the search committee was forced to make many tough decisions
with over three hundred and fifty applicants for this position, we have had to pass over many candidates with excellent qualifications
these decisions should not be read as judgments on your qualifications
our decisions have been especially difficult and painful
compiling a short list of applicants was not an easy task
as you can imagine, the process of selection was extremely difficult
and it was difficult, to say the least, and selecting finalists has been very difficult

don't do or say that to that

Which freedoms would I most readily give away?

the assumption is you *choose* the identity you construct
and you cannot avoid it ultimately

every word calling
upon the wisdom
of those assembled

some among you will deem this a lofty pursuit

Madam, and madam – is the nature of my criminality not entirely mine own

I don't practice release I *visualize* my essence I don't project it

in bed rushing
and in conflict
insurance against personality loss

why couldn't we all have been more . . .

you've got my hair

were it not for her appearance these questions could not have been asked

let's switch places

don't say no like I do

"csi"

almost all usage books recognize the legitimacy of me,
especially in speech

as a sort of universal syntax error

but, in truth, we've spoiled everything

and things shift
like boundaries
and prices fix
like identities

I was never unexpectedly addressed
by the sound of my own voice

and felt that a detriment

2.

yup yup yup

that's me marking a territory

3.

the men are uniformly large
and business class
be shrouded in blue

and ink a thanks

for the impact

she seems to be crying

4.

this terminal marks the end of the west

plucker or ears – she made mine perk up

his eyes were wide with inwardness

5.

in Ottawa they skate on the

I could sense his readiness, had I time

we are all competing for limited resources

or making a similar attempt

6.

he appears to be married, to be waiting
for someone, to be
scratching his head
running his fingers through his hair
looking down the street
he's wiping his nose

7.

these words signal
the end
of my character
assassination

I am grasping what I imagine
is
the heroic eclipse - -

a "receiver"

a cross between a handgun and a tea towel

those are my crosshairs

his high anxiety

my churlish farewell

8.

and it garnered a major reappraisal
of a very basic gesture
to even think
at that moment

of mechanical humming of wheels of vitality
in me

I'm sorry if I have let you down, if the book I have chosen
has. If you have been let down, sorry. The book, I have
chosen it. Nevertheless for it, sorry to let you down, I'm
sorry if. If down has you the book left, sorry so sorry. If
has top-down schema the let book down, say down, put it
down, and sorry to you now to take it up. If I or we or the book
has let you down let you take it down or put you down or
put you I'm sorry.

ABOUT THE AUTHOR

A native of New York, Linda Russo has published several chapbooks, including *o going out* (Potes & Poets) and *secret silent plan* (curricle patterns). She earned her M.F.A from Emerson College and her Ph.D. from the University at Buffalo and has published several essays on contemporary women poets. She teaches presently at the University of Oklahoma.

Also from Chax Press

Glen Mott, *Analects on a Chinese Screen*
Bruce Andrews, *Swoon Noir*
Tim Peterson, *Since I Moved In*
Jefferson Carter, *Sentimental Blue*
Joe Amato, *Under Virga*
Charles Borkhuis, *After Image*
David Abel, *Black Valentine*
Paul Naylor, *Arranging Nature*
Kass Fleisher, *Accidental Species*
Tenney Nathanson, *Erased Art*
Heather Nagami, *Hostile*
Linh Dinh, *American Tatts*
Beverly Dahlen, *A-Reading Spicer & 18 Sonnets*
Elizabeth Treadwell, *Chantry*
Allison Cobb, *Born Two*

For our many additional titles please visit our web site: http://chax.org/

Chax Press is supported by the Tucson Pima Arts Council and by the Arizona Commission on the Arts with funding from the State of Arizona and the National Endowment for the Arts.

TUCSON PIMA ARTS COUNCIL

Arizona Commission on the Arts

NATIONAL ENDOWMENT FOR THE ARTS